facing maria

MARIA HUTCHISON

BALBOA.
PRESS
A DIVISION OF HAY HOUSE

Balboa Press books may be ordered through booksellers or by contacting:

Balboa Press
A Division of Hay House
1663 Liberty Drive
Bloomington, IN 47403
www.balboapress.com.au
1 (877) 407-4847

Because of the dynamic nature of the Internet, any web addresses or
links contained in this book may have changed since publication and
may no longer be valid. The views expressed in this work are solely those
of the author and do not necessarily reflect the views of the publisher,
and the publisher hereby disclaims any responsibility for them.

The author of this book does not dispense medical advice or prescribe the use
of any technique as a form of treatment for physical, emotional, or medical
problems without the advice of a physician, either directly or indirectly. The
intent of the author is only to offer information of a general nature to help
you in your quest for emotional and spiritual well-being. In the event you use
any of the information in this book for yourself, which is your constitutional
right, the author and the publisher assume no responsibility for your actions.

Print information available on the last page.

ISBN: 978-1-5043-1735-1 (sc)
ISBN: 978-1-5043-1736-8 (e)

Balboa Press rev. date: 03/27/2019

Contents

Facing Maria – Overview

Have you ever wondered who you were meant to be?

Have you considered or spent time trying to work out what exactly you were put on this earth for? Has your thinking led you to wonder who you may have been, or what you were going to be, if a particular experience didn't happen? Do you wish you were born at a different time, in a different place, had never had that accident, suffered that abuse, met/married that person?

Well I have. I realise that for a large part of my adult life I have wondered who I was meant to be. I have used excuse after excuse as to why I haven't been able to stay in a job for more than 2 years, why I have had failed relationship after relationship, why I have used sex addiction as a crutch, why I have spent so much of my life overweight, why I can never seem to stay happy, and why I can't save money.

Interestingly each and every one of those excuses has been valid enough to be accepted; not just by myself, but also by many of the people I spend time with. Another interesting point is that every one of those excuses involves what "someone" else being accountable for why I did not move forward as I wished in my life!

So here I am – four days before my 41st birthday and my world has turned upside down. I have been given an incredible gift of insight. The gift of acceptance and inner knowing that I AM who I was born to be! I am exactly whom I am meant to be and that it was I who created every single one of these experiences so I could fully relish this moment. I can totally experience the joy of having my eyes open, the truth revealed and so I can fully absorb the feeling of freedom that has come my way.

I was born and brought into this world to know FREEDOM; and to help others who find themselves trapped and restricted to find freedom for themselves, allowing their inner mojo or essence to be released from the binds of oppression and restriction. To achieve this, the only true way of knowing and appreciating freedom is to also to experience what it takes to have no freedom, to be restricted and to have no choice, to be bound, tied and gagged.

I have found so many different ways of restricting myself from the experience of freedom throughout my life, that even I am amazed at the lengths I have gone to so that I can experience the opposite end of the freedom spectrum!

Let me share with you some of the lengths I have gone to in order so that I can now know freedom and some of the lessons I have learnt along the way!

Preface

Sometimes it is easier to start at the end rather than the beginning when it comes to issues of higher consciousness and understanding ourselves. It is with this in mind and with the intent of helping you, the reader, have a better understanding of the context and purpose of this book that I chose to begin at the end rather than the beginning...

At some time before 1972 (I am not sure how long before) a higher conscious version of my "Self" sat down with what I call my higher council and agreed that my "Self" would come to earth with the sole purpose to help other souls experience inner happiness and to know joy and freedom while doing so.

In accordance with my choice and negotiations with this higher council I was born into a human form on 5 May 1972. From that moment on I have been living my purpose, like I believe all humans are.

In order to know freedom and be in a position to help others find their own freedom, my higher council deemed it important for me to know and experience the opposite of freedom first. And so for the first 40 years on this earth that is essentially the experience I have had. In the relative world we live in it can be no other way. We cannot know light without knowing and having a concept of darkness, nor can we appreciate positive without knowledge of negative, there is no black without white.

My truth is that for many years I did not understand this concept. As you read through the following chapters you will understand that this belief or concept is certainly not one I recognised or owned when I was born, nor is it a belief system I was born into. This belief has come about from many years of exploration, pain, happiness and challenges. For many years I looked back on my life and judged many of my experiences as negative, some traumatic, some unjustified, many privileged and some wonderfully blessed.

Despite the original agreement of my life purpose, my "Self" could not understand why I had been *put through* or *had to endure* many of the experiences of my childhood. I firmly believed I had no choice about what *happened to me* and that I most definitely didn't ask for any of it. I spent many years blaming and outsourcing responsibility onto other people, accidents, religious beliefs, where I was born – all manner of things. To have suggested that I was responsible and had chosen these things in my life was just way too much for me to accept.

I was brought up to see myself as separate to God and to believe that my life was given to me in order to please Him. I believed that He had a purpose for me and that He loved me. I was born into a privileged family in the sense that we were part of God's family on earth. Trying to reconcile this with the experiences of my life was a challenge – how could He allow this to happen to me? Why did He make me so bad if all I had to do was spend my life trying to be something different in order to please Him? All the while laying all responsibility and control onto a God that resided outside of me.

What I will share with you in this book is a result of many pathways I have taken in order to know and experience freedom in my own life. Ultimately this has come about through the relative experience of knowing what it is to **not** feel free to be myself nor to think, dream or choose from my own experience or heart.

There have been so many experiences that have led me to this current state of being I find myself in now. There has been no single magic solution. My transformation has taken years of therapy, self-reflection, trial and error, pain, sorrow, joy and elation. My current circumstances have come about simply through experience. It can be no other way – experiencing myself as myself. I have been guided and helped by so many people; wise words have been spoken, enlightened words have been written, remarkable lives have been lived; and all the opposite of that too!

To say that it has been simply about changing my beliefs makes it sound so uncomplicated and easy. Yet ultimately that is how simple it has been!

The path to uncovering the beliefs that have kept me bound is what has taken the time; it has often been painful and has required immense self-reflection, honesty and often a lot of pushing and encouragement from others.

Now I fully see and know at a soul level that I chose this life, and that each and every experience I have been through in my life has been for this purpose – that I might know and appreciate freedom and bring this gift to others.

Throughout this book I have included a piece at the end of each chapter which outlines the self-limiting belief that I uncovered was the key to keeping me bound and preventing me experiencing freedom in each of these areas of my life. As you will see often there was more than one belief that was limiting my healing and progress.

I have also included the affirmation that I used to help me heal and to change the belief to what I now believe about myself.

Affirmations have been, and still play an instrumental role in my life. As a human being I have 50,000-60,000 thoughts a day. Many of these are unconscious and, as for most people, many of them were negative. When I first started doing affirmations I certainly didn't believe what I was saying and struggled with that. I have proved in my own experience, and witnessed it for many others too, that when I consciously affirm and replace even 10 of my 50,000 thoughts a day, my life changes. I know I am constantly creating my reality by my thoughts and beliefs. By ensuring that I consciously make some of those thoughts and beliefs positive and about whom I want to be, results in exactly what I experience.

For me, the simplest way to make sustainable life changes is to have the courage and openness to go within and really examine what I am thinking and believing. I know and understand that behind and beneath any behaviours and actions sit my thoughts and beliefs. In order to change how I act I first need to change how I think and what I believe.

And finally in my preface it is important for me to add a disclaimer as well. I have in no way finished exploring myself, nor do I suggest that I understand all the answers for everyone or everything. There is so much I am still learning about myself, so many beliefs that I am still discovering and challenging, many of which are so ingrained and have been around

for so long, that I am not currently conscious of their limiting impacts.

So as you read the following pages please know that these are MY lessons to date and my understanding of MYSELF so far. It is in no way intended to be neither an attack nor an inference of blame on anyone or anything from my past.

I write this book with the single intent of bringing awareness to all who read the pages that follow. It is my desire that we all might know freedom to be our authentic, genuine and unique selves. I share this story of my journey, trusting that this book will leave you knowing without a doubt that this is not only possible, but it is also a fantastic place to be!

Freedom Within Religion

The best place to start is with my birth family. It is impossible for me to separate family from religion due to the strong beliefs that I grew up amongst.

It is a well-known fact that each and every baby that comes into the world comes in totally dependent on others for everything. It is part of the ebb and flow of nature that we come into this life as perfect little beings and we are totally reliant on outside influences for our wellbeing and survival. It is in these early years of development that we learn the most, and it is also the time that many of our values and beliefs are established and grounded for the rest of our life. This is quite ironic really as it is the time when we have the least ability to say or know what we want and we know the least!

So the family I chose to come into the world with and who could offer me the most learning about freedom, was a family based in a small town on the west coast of the south island in New Zealand. I selected a family who could teach me a lot about the constraints of life in order that I can now know and appreciate freedom.

My mother and father were humble folk and both devout Christians. The belief they followed was steeped in tradition and fear. Taking no name, the fellowship observes the New Testament teachings of Jesus. My mother was brought up in the fellowship and my father was introduced to the belief from his early teenage years. In the town where I grew up there was a population of 6,000. Other than our family of seven (Mum, Dad and five children), there were only three other households who held the same belief that we worshipped with. The only other children were two younger boys – 7 and 8 years my junior.

Our extended family of approximately thirty-five cousins on Mum's side, and ten on Dad's side, predominately lived in the one city about four hours drive away and we visited them often. The majority of these families and cousins were also involved in the fellowship and followed the same beliefs and lifestyles that we did.

Some of the constraints of the belief that set us apart from others were as follows:

- We had no TV or radio.
- Women had long hair, which was not coloured or cut, and was to be worn up in either a bun or pulled away from the face.

- Women did not wear trousers, jewellery or make-up.
- Sunday was a day of rest and worship.
- Fellowship meetings were held in members' houses three times per week, usually lasting approximately 1 hour.
- There were no formal church buildings as such due to the teachings of Jesus that God does not dwell in temples made of stone but in our hearts. Gospel meetings where non-members were invited to attend and listen to the preaching were held in school halls and other hired facilities.
- Preachers went out as in the New Testament (directed by God, they owned no worldly possessions, took no wage, were not educated in preaching or teaching, never married and went out into areas in pairs, staying in the homes of members within the fellowship).

The teachings were all referenced back to the scripture although the unwritten laws and rules were many and deep. A definite life of self-denial, humility, and unworthiness was encouraged. Many of the beliefs were backed up by the interpretation of the scriptures. Others were just "known" and to question them was to show a lack of faith.

Knowing freedom amongst this belief, as you can imagine, was a challenge. A perfect environment to learn what freedom is not.

The teachings came predominantly from the preacher's and the elders amongst the church. My parents reiterated these teachings to us children and tried their very best to live according to them. I was taught how to think, what was right, what was wrong, what was good, what was bad according to the teachings of the fellowship. I was told what to wear, where to go and not go, who to mix with and who not to mix with, what to say, how to pray and fundamentally that this was "the only way" to know God and that we were His chosen few.

In essence, living in the fellowship was a safety zone. I knew what the rules were, I knew what was expected of me, and I knew what made other people happy and therefore how to get their approval. I believed that if I could just live within the rules then God would take care of me and I would be happy. In fact, God had a plan for me, and it was just up to me to obey it, fit in and to live according to His teachings and I would know peace; both here on Earth and in Heaven later.

I learnt very early on in my life how to live according to rules. I knew the length of my skirt that was appropriate. I knew that if I wore stockings to our meetings – even when it was really hot – I would meet God's approval and the approval of the preachers and elders of the church. I knew that by playing the piano and singing hymns made my parents happy. I was constantly aware of others' reactions to my behaviour so I learnt to control it very well.

I professed and gave my life to God when I was thirteen as I knew this was "the right" thing to do. My father had drowned a few months earlier and I wanted so much to make my mother and my late father proud of me, professing was a sure way of doing it. I had also been assured that God was the one who could heal the hurt I was feeling and could answer my questions and concerns.[1]

I honestly believe that I did have a relationship with God at this time. I prayed morning and evening and spent time reading the bible each day and tried to live according to what I had been taught was "right". I tried desperately to understand how Dad's death was part of His plan; but ultimately I just wanted to make the pain go away, to make Mum happy, and find some happiness and peace for myself.

Was this a choice of *free will* that I was part of this fellowship? Did I feel free to serve a God who I knew as my own? Did I feel worthy of being myself? Did I love and approve of myself and know that I was acceptable in God's sight?

---

[1]   Professing essentially meant an outward declaration of my inward belief and commitment to God. It meant that I chose to give myself, and my life to living according to the principles and guidelines of the church and belief. It meant that my life was no longer my own, that I have given it in service to God. As a professing member of the faith I was able to speak, pray and share my experiences in the fellowship meetings.

Not really, but I knew what was expected of me as a *professing person*. I knew how to get approval from those around me who I believed were closer to God than I was, and who taught us the rules.

I *knew* that I had a choice; in fact it was called "making your choice" when you professed to serve God. I also knew, however, that according to what I had been told and the basis of our belief, if I made a choice not to serve God then I would never be happy and would most certainly be going to hell. I was so confused and mixed up with my dad dying that the last thing I wanted was to be heading to somewhere even worse when this life was all over.

Finding Freedom...

Challenging my religious upbringing and the ingrained teachings has been one of the hardest lessons in my life. Really asking what do I believe? Challenging why I believe this, what is the evidence I have for my beliefs? Is it what I think I should believe? Is it something I am afraid not to believe, or is it something I know within my inner being is what I believe or feels like the truth for me?

I was asked by a life coach to do an exercise on being versus doing and the process was to ask myself what do I do that makes me happy? At the time I was 40-years-old and had done many years of self-healing, self-development and self-help work and yet this simple question was extremely difficult for me to answer. When I asked myself what makes me happy my thoughts would run through so many filters inside my head that were based around others and my responsibilities. Was I allowed to enjoy this? What would people say if I did this? Is this a responsible thing to be doing? Is it what a "good" person would do?

I kept coming up with a teaching from my childhood; that in order to know true JOY it stood for Jesus First, Others Next and Yourself Last! So as you can imagine trying to get to what made me happy was a long and challenging road! I have done very little in my life purely because it makes me happy!

My experience of religion is all about others opinions and/or others interpretation of what is right and/or wrong. Essentially, all scripture is written by another person at some stage in history and therefore there is an element of interpretation in it all by default. There is often no room for genuine self-discovery or experiencing what is honestly best for you as this could well challenge the interpretations of others and make them "wrong". Organised religion of any denomination has a black and a white approach and misses out on so much of what is in-between.

My experience of religion also is about dependence. It's not about asking what makes me happy or what makes me feel closest to my creator; it has been more about what makes others happy and needing to have confirmation from others at all times that I am on the right track.

Growing up with the bondage of a fear and guilt-based religion is all consuming. Not having the freedom to choose what I wanted to wear, where I wanted to go, who I wanted to be friends with, who I wanted to marry, what I could say and so many other things.

It is no wonder now that I experience a sense of utter delight and appreciation when I get up in the morning and decide what to wear based on how I am feeling rather than who I will be seeing that day or where I am going! The choice to wear make-up or not wear make-up makes my heart swell each morning. Deciding that I would rather not spend time in the company of a person as I feel unsafe around them or I have nothing in common with them is liberating! Saying "no thanks" to an invitation to spend time with someone I have no respect for is such freedom!

It has taken some real inner reflection, challenging and changing of my beliefs to be at a point where I can honestly say I am genuinely proud of each of my three children, and the wonderful souls they are without any sense of guilt or shame about them having three different fathers and two being born out of wedlock. Not just for me but of course for them as well! It has meant that my relationship with each child is unique and comes from a true place of love. I trust that they in turn will know and appreciate the freedom they can choose throughout their lives.

Experiencing the most wonderful loving husband and a relationship wherein I am free to be myself is something I value more each day. It is still such a novelty for me to really test the boundaries and show my inner fears, dreams and secrets and I find myself delighted when I look into the eyes of my husband, and see that he still loves me and does not judge me for any of it!

My marriage is something I am in all honesty, only beginning to appreciate for its full beauty and wonder, as it has taken a while to let go of the childhood belief that I have sinned greatly because I have been married and divorced before meeting my husband. Valuing my marriage and my husband and truly honouring the union of our lives is an ongoing learning for me. Totally trusting him, communicating openly and freely is something that I always desperately try to do each and every day.

I am aware that I still carry some unwanted and restricting beliefs that are deeply rooted in my early years. However, what I am so thankful for now is the enlightenment that this experience gave me that I might know freedom. There is no way I can truly value and experience freedom if I have not experienced bondage and restriction. There is no way to know light blue if one hasn't experienced dark blue, joy without sorrow, nor good without bad!

I am grateful that I have the freedom to follow my heart and explore my spirituality! I am grateful that

I have the freedom to challenge my beliefs and test them and question whether they are still serving me. How liberating it can be to change a belief that no longer serves my best interest and replace it with one that brings freedom and brings me closer to living my true purpose!

And ultimately this does not mean denying God or a higher power; in fact it means becoming closer to Him/Her/It/Self/Source!

SELF-LIMITING BELIEFS:

"True Joy comes from putting Jesus First, Others Next and Yourself Last".
"There is only ONE way".
"You cannot know happiness without God in your life".
"Family comes first".
"One must honour one's mother/father".
"Secrets are best kept within the family".

AFFIRMATIONS FOR FREEDOM:

"I affirm it is safe for me to follow my heart and explore my spirituality".
"I love and approve of myself and act always in accordance with my highest good".
"I am enough as I am"
"I am source, all I need is within me now".
"I give thanks for my freedom to speak my truth and follow my heart".

Freedom Through Loss

My memories of my father are of a strong, passionate man and a devout Christian.

He was born as the third son in a family of four boys to my grandparents who had both migrated from the Shetland Islands to New Zealand in the early 1900's.

My grandfather was a fisherman who had left home when he was twelve on a fishing boat in order to support his mother, brothers and sisters. His father was a fisherman who drowned when my grandfather was five years old. My memories of my grandad are of a strong, opinionated man with a history of doing it tough and surviving. He could, and did, hold a grudge for years and yet was a perfect gentleman and knew how to "treat a lady". One of my fondest memories of my grandfather is that after sixty years of marriage to my grandma, he never once looked in her handbag! Even after she died he was unable to go through her handbag to sort through her things. This symbolism of deep and utter respect for his wife still means something to me today and I thank him for this memory.

My grandmother was the epitome of a lady. She has been, and continues to be, one of my biggest mentors and heroes. Five feet tall, whichever way you looked at her she had the most wonderful kind heart and soul and was a true, loving, caring, inspiring woman and grandmother. Her patience and non-judgemental approach to others has long been a quality I admire and seek to emulate.

My father grew up with fishing in his blood despite the fact that he grew up on a dairy farm and studied to be a diesel mechanic. His passion and love for the sea would not be silenced and regardless of his success and ability with mechanics, and the stability that such a profession would give him rather than fishing, being at sea won out and he held many jobs working for others on their boats. Necessity took him back on occasions to working as a mechanic but, according to my mother, he was never as happy as he was when fishing. Although as a couple they struggled to make ends meet financially, and he could earn more money in a secure land-based role, it was not where his heart lay. He eventually fulfilled his dream and ambition and owned his own boat "The Rita 1".

Fishing on the west coast of the south island of New Zealand was not an easy game. Wild weather and a rough industry; it was important that you loved it in order to survive. Dad was the president of the local fishermen's club and respected by many despite having a very different lifestyle to many of the local fishermen.

Dad's spiritual beliefs meant that he never fished on Sundays, as this was a day of rest and a day spent with the family. He also didn't drink or smoke or swear so he certainly stood out from the others. I understand that some in the community knew him as "Christian Bill" as everyone knew what he stood for, and regardless of who was with him on the boat at any time, he always read his Bible each morning and night and prayed. He made no secret of his beliefs and yet made no judgement of others for their lifestyle, and so our house was often the location of a fishermen's committee meeting, or the gathering place of a few fishermen as they fixed their nets or made use of dad's mechanical skills to have repairs done on their cars or boats.

It is perfectly apt that it was whilst he was out fishing, on his own boat on his own, that he breathed his last breath on this earth. He was only forty-three when his boat was capsized by a freak wave as he crossed the bar into the Westport harbour on 16th July 1985. I was thirteen years old.

I remember the night very vividly. It was a rainy dark cloudy afternoon and I got very wet as I rode my bike home from school. I was in my first year of high school and so pleased that I got a new 10-speed bike for Christmas that year. It was my first "new" bike in my life and I had talked Dad into buying it for me although Mum had said we couldn't afford it.

My mother's parents were staying with us at the time. Both sets of my grandparents lived four hours away in Nelson and so they would come to visit and stay with us for 1-2 weeks at a time.

We lived in the state-housing section of Westport; our neighbours were predominately single parents and beneficiaries who were in commissioned housing. Mum and Dad (and the bank) owned our house though and in our cul-de-sac there were another 2 or 3 homeowners.

Mum was at the kitchen sink making dinner when Dad called through on the CB radio about 5pm to say that he was going to be later in today as he was on his own and needed to clean the fish coming up the river before unloading and making his way home. This was the first day Dad had been able to go out fishing for 2 weeks, as the weather had been so bad.

My 18-year-old elder brother answered the phone at home at approximately 5:20pm from a friend of the family who called to ask whether Dad was in as there was a boat tipped over on the bar. Her husband had been called to go out with a local policeman in his jet boat to help.

My brother got off the phone and told us what the call was about. In an instant I remember crying out

"It's him!" I saw Mum's ashen face and then as she tried to calm me down I saw my brother run out to his car. I started to follow, but was stopped by Mum from following him out into the rain.

There began five days of craziness until Saturday 20th July 1985 when Dad's body was found washed up on the beach by a local schoolboy.

My last conversation with Dad was on the previous Sunday night. I had approached Dad and asked him if I could have my hair cut into a fringe. Women within the church did not have their hair cut or coloured and so my long hair hung in curly ringlets. When Dad asked why I wanted my haircut I explained, in the best way I knew how at thirteen, that I was the only girl in the whole school who did not have a fringe!

My father's response was simple and to the point... "Maria, you have to learn that you don't do things in life because everyone else is doing it. You must learn to follow your heart and do what you believe is right for you". I promptly huffed my way up from the table and into my bedroom, declaring to my sister that 'Dad has no idea about life and was being completely unreasonable' and a whole raft of other disappointed venting!

It wasn't until many years later that I realised what a gift he gave me, how wise and precious those words were and have come to be in my life! When someone close to you dies it is the ultimate in loss of freedom.

The experience of having my father die when I was a 13-year-old girl taught me so much. No longer could I check in with him, get his approval or ask him for guidance or advice. How did he gain his faith? Did he ever doubt? What were his struggles? What would he do? What did he mean when he said and did this or that? My memories of my father are based around recollections, imaginings, what others have said about him, what I think others said about him; not based on my reality at all. Memories don't allow for growth either and this is one of the biggest bondages I have known with not having Dad around.

Later in life after I had left the church and had my hair cut, my Grandmother commented to me one day, "Your father will be turning in his grave with disappointment if he could see you Maria". Would he really? It was 5-6 years since he had died; he couldn't know what I had been through, he didn't know what it was like to lose a parent at thirteen, to move schools, to have to look after your mum who was grieving and lost, to have your brother and sister leave home, to see the struggle of your younger brothers as they tried to understand what it all meant, nor to realise that I was a victim of sexual abuse...

Dad was not here for any of this so I was left to imagine what his response would be which totally discounts the growth that he would have gone through if he was still here experiencing life alongside of us!

I have grieved for my father in many different ways over the years. I have missed him during the big moments of my life – I miss him for my children. I have been angry with him, disillusioned with him, tried to talk to him, and told myself lies about him in order to make it hurt less. I have also blamed him and his death for many of my mistakes and life experiences.

Finding Freedom...

Only now do I realise that his death taught me so much about freedom. I choose to believe that he knew the kind of freedom that I have been seeking all my life. I admire his ability to follow his heart into the fishing industry but not lose his purpose and his belief and faith. I respect that this would have required a great commitment for him to remain "faithful", essentially in a town of 6,000 people who didn't think or believe what he did.

Whether it's a belief that I agree with or not, it is Dad's confidence and his ability to stay true to himself and to freely live the life he chose that I respect.

For me my lesson was in the freedom that comes from communication and observation. Not having the freedom to ask questions, to learn from others' experiences, to check in with others for their advice, to see their growth and change, and to learn from their mistakes and victories is the restricted. We can only learn so much from books or others' accounts of a person's life or our own memories. It is through our relationship with others that we learn the most about ourselves and have the opportunity to experience ourselves as ourselves.

I have learnt to make the most of people I have around me now that I admire, who have come into my life to teach me something or to be taught something from me. I attempt to make the most of it in every relationship, in every communication and interaction with another human being, to really experience being present with them. I try to ensure that I give each interaction the respect it deserves, give myself permission and freedom to be myself, and to allow them to be their true self as well as we learn and grow together. I don't always succeed at this but it is certainly something I continually strive for.

It always surprises me when I talk with my brothers and sisters about their memories of Dad surrounding his life and death and just how different our "stories" are. We all remember Dad in a different way, we remember that night differently and our lives have been affected by not having him around in differing ways as well.

I have learnt to challenge some of my memories and or assumptions that do not serve me well and that have kept me bound in negativity, and I am grateful that I can now create my own story in order that I might know freedom!

SELF-LIMITING BELIEFS:

"I have to make my father proud"
"I need to prove myself and that I am worthy of being part of the family".
"Do not let the family name down".
"No-one in our family has done..."
"Dad would be so ashamed of me".

AFFIRMATIONS FOR FREEDOM:

"I give thanks that I no longer need to prove myself to anyone".
"I am 100% responsible for my own happiness – and allow others the same freedom".
"I am surrounded by love and support".
"I belong"
"I am enough as I am"

Sexual Freedom

Interestingly I have used the avenue of sex to learn most of my lessons about freedom during my life. Quite fitting when you consider how taboo sex is even in society today. It is the perfect avenue for learning lessons on freedom and bondage as it is rarely spoken about without guilt, shame, and judgement or with a true sense of comfort!

My learning around sex started early in life when at the age of around 4-years-old I started to be sexually abused by my maternal grandfather. Bondage and restriction started immediately. I was alone with my grandfather as he was looking after me whilst my mother was out. We had been playing a game with a table tennis ball where he would hide it and I had to find it. Innocent enough until he put the ball down inside his pants.

I don't know if it was an inner knowing at the time or whether it was his prompting, but I knew there was something about this that didn't feel right or good to me. That is evident of course by the fact that I knew enough to know that I was not free to tell anyone about it!

I was abused by my grandfather for approximately eight years. For some of this time we were living in the same house but predominately it was when they came for visits or we visited them. The sexual abuse did not just happen behind closed doors or in the bedroom, he would often have his hand up my skirt in a room filled with people as I sat on his knee. Sometimes in a room full of people singing hymns! He would pull me into a hug that was too long, press his body against mine and cause me to feel his penis when there were others around and all disguised as the acts of a loving grandfather. He was also a well-respected elder of the church and very much the patriarch of the family.

During this time I was vulnerable and an easy target for other perpretrators as well and experienced further violations from another two individuals. I never told anyone about this and to be perfectly honest didn't know that it was wrong because like the "love" that Grandad was showing me, it made me feel special.

So from the age of 4-years-old I was caught up in the bondage of secrets. Secrets of others, on behalf of others, for others and about sex!

It all became very confused in my mind as our parents never openly spoke about sex and yet we knew it was wrong, and also because Grandad was an elder of the church, and so I moved even further away from freedom and from my essence of who I really was. I didn't know! I knew what I was expected to be, and for a large part I lived that as I knew how to make people happy but I certainly didn't feel connected to what I was living.

Some of the strongest messages my grandfather gave to me through the years of abuse was that I was too fat and ugly to ever get a man later in life so I should make the most of it from him. He also said that he was the only one who really loved me and understood me because no one else loved me like he did or in the same way.

One of my biggest sorrows now as I reflect back, is that I embraced this inner belief for such a big part of my childhood. I interacted with my father for the few short years I had him from the perspective that he didn't really love me because he didn't do what Grandad did. I have memories of climbing into bed beside him when I was having an asthma attack and Dad would breathe deeply with me to help it pass. I recall lifting up my little nightie so he might touch me in the same way as Grandad had so I could know that he really loved me, and I felt such deep hurt and sorrow when he pulled my nightie down again!

Sexual abuse destroyed my perception of my true self. It tainted my relationships with those around me and damaged my ability to trust; not just others but myself.

The physical sexual abuse from my grandfather stopped not long before my father died when I was about twelve and was more conscious of my body and the fact that it was not normal. The mental abuse from Grandad didn't really stop though for many years and I managed to carry it on as well by creating my sex addiction.

When I was 18-years-old I returned to study to become a nanny. Early in our training we were taught to identify if a child had, or was being sexually abused. This was genuinely the first time that I realised the extent of what had happened to me and the reality that I had been abused. This also came with another layer of guilt and fear when we were taught the statistics that showed that those who have been abused often then abuse others! That was extremely confronting for me considering here I was training to look after children! Training to be a nanny was the catalyst for me seeking help and was when I first entered therapy. I sought out the help of a counsellor at the time and with her help I came to understand myself at a new level. I began the journey of challenging, understanding and appreciating the impact that sexual abuse had had on **my** life, **my** thoughts and **my** beliefs.

I lost my virginity around this time as I had stopped going to the church and started going out to pubs and clubs with other students for the first time. I didn't know how to say no to a male if he asked me to dance let alone how to say no to him if he wanted to take me home to bed! I slept with so many different men during the next few years, not all of them safe, not all of them people I liked. So, I was now keeping secrets about sex at a whole new level!

The paradox of addiction is that it is so restricting and disabling because it creates the belief that there is no choice. Addiction offers no choice and yet I felt and looked to those around me like I was expressing my sexuality and that I was open and free! The guilt and shame I felt from the sex abuse was intensified by the guilt and shame I felt about the sex addiction. It was a vicious cycle.

I constantly sought out men to have sex with to stop the voice inside my head that was telling me I was too fat and ugly for anyone to love me. However, once I had sex with them I felt ashamed of what I had done and believed that if they really knew me they wouldn't love me anyway. In order not to get hurt anymore I would seek out someone else to have sex with to make me feel that I was loveable. All I learnt was I was "fuckable" but until I loved myself I was indeed pretty hard to love!

The abuse that happened to me as a child was so insidious because it shaped so much of what I believed about myself and my self-worth. I don't think any form of abuse is better than another as I see that mental and physical abuse have just as devastating effects as sexual abuse on a person. The outer and the inner, that which is hidden and that which is public, the good and the bad, the softness and the hardness; all of me was impacted.

I now understand that many abuse survivors go on to develop and maintain addiction in some form or another, which is of course a way of continuing the abuse. The loss of self-worth, the loss of clarity, the confusion, and lack of trust, anger and sadness develops into a fear. A fear of freedom! A paralysing fear that takes over – who will I be? Who was I meant to be? What if people knew what I was really thinking? What if I said what I really thought? What if they find out? What if I got angry – could I stop myself? What if I started crying and then couldn't stop? What if what Grandad said was right? What if what they said was wrong? Did they really say that? Did it really happen at all? Who would believe me?

These thoughts and fears consumed my every action and so the easiest and best thing to do, and what would often happen, is I would turn back to religion, or to rules, or my comfort zone! I have returned twice throughout my adult life to the same religion or rules that bound me in the beginning. I realise now that in both instances it was for safety.

In my early thirties I manifested this same approach in a different way by getting into a relationship with someone who was really controlling and with whom I didn't feel I could be myself. For a while this gave me safety, at least I knew what the rules were, I knew how to make him happy and therefore I figured I knew how to keep safe.

Safe from myself, safe from ever having to really feel these frightening feelings, safe from having to feel too much at all.

Safety was survival.

Finding Freedom...

Learning to separate sex from love and approval was instrumental to me in healing from my sex addiction.

This was not easy to do as it meant opening up initially and sharing the secret. Not just the secret about the sexual abuse, but also the even bigger secret about how I had chosen to deal with the memories and the pain – by creating an addiction to sexual acting out.

This journey led me to spend three months in a rehabilitation facility in 1994 where I was admitted for my sex addiction and where as a 22-year-old woman I was once again in the minority, because of my youth and also because of the nature of my addiction and the fact that I was a woman.

I spent some years seeking help from 12-step programs and also back into the church to help me stay clean and stop me from "acting out".

However, over the years my sex addiction has remained a part of my identity and an avenue that I used to prove my self-worth, to beat up on myself, and one of my ways of coping with the stresses and struggles in life. My sense of freedom from my addiction came when I was truly able to see it for what it was; it was a coping mechanism for dealing with my thoughts and beliefs about my unworthiness and my lack of self-worth. It was keeping me in bondage to the old identity. I used it to essentially escape myself.

To know freedom from any addiction is incredibly empowering. To realise that you have a choice as to whether you "use" your drug of choice or whether you act on your impulses is so refreshing to begin with, and then when you can start to make other choices about how to act is a freedom like no other.

Challenging my beliefs about sex, about how sexual abuse had defined my identity, and unravelling the link with self-love, self-respect and sex, was imperative to the freedom I now know.

I think the biggest lesson I learnt from my sex addiction in finding my freedom, is about the secrets that we keep that keep us sick and/or stuck. Initially it was keeping the secret of my Grandfather's abuse that allowed the abuse to continue rather than me receiving support as a child. It then developed into keeping the secrets of my thinking, my actions around sex that allowed the addiction to develop, grow and ultimately define my identity.

Opening up and sharing my secrets has been incredibly freeing; not just for myself, but for many within my family and my circle of associates as well. I now appreciate the freedom that comes from living free from addictive acting out.

SELF-LIMITING BELIEFS:

"I am not worthy".
"Once an addict, always an addict".
"I need to prove to others that I am loveable".
"I am too fat and ugly to be loved"
"My secrets keep me safe".

AFFIRMATIONS FOR FREEDOM:

"I give thanks I no longer need to act out or prove myself to anyone".
"I am enough as I am".
"I love and approve of myself".
"I act always in accordance with my highest good – I am love and I am loved".
"I give thanks that my self-worth is no longer dependant on anything outside of myself".

Freedom In And With My Own Body

Freedom in respect of my body is an interesting concept. I have certainly known the opposite!

I am truly not sure when I started to carry my issues around on my body. I don't know when the abuse, feelings and thoughts I couldn't release started transforming into extra weight, but according to my memory I have always been "fat". Maybe this did start to happen by Grandad's messaging while he was abusing me, although as I look back at photos of myself throughout my childhood I realise that I was in fact not as overweight as I have believed.

What I do know is that I grew up in an environment where it was admired to be self-deprecating, to believe that we were born sinners, that there was nothing attractive about ourselves without God. If I was ever told that I was beautiful just the way I was, I certainly never heard it over the negative thoughts and talk that I heard.

Using my body to create restraint was another way that I have operated in the past. Creating extra weight around myself literally kept people at a distance. Even through the years of my rampant sex addiction I felt a sense of safety because of my size. I believed that people saw my size before they saw anything else. I also knew that if someone took me home to have sex they knew I was big before we left the bar so there was no way they would expect anything different when we got home.

What was interesting about my attitude towards my size is that I never let others know that it was an issue for me. The weight just kept piling on and I never sought help. I went on very few diets even when I was at my heaviest because I honestly had no interest in being smaller.

I look back now and I see that the weight limited my life in so many ways. It also kept me bound in other unhealthy ways too; I constantly had to prove that I was good enough. "If you just get to know me", my inner voice screamed, "I am quite a nice person but you have to look past this fat and ugly exterior first."

I was constantly abusing my body; sexually with my addiction, mentally with my inner negative self-talk and physically with the food that I was putting into it. I had no respect for myself or my body and therefore spent little time caring for myself in a healthy way.

What I did do though was cover it up well with clothing. I wanted to look good and so brought lots of expensive clothes and outfits that of course were a challenge to get in my size! I believed that if I presented as being happy in my skin, and looked like I was doing well then no one would ever really know the torment inside.

Not being able to be truthful about myself or my feelings, concerns and fears kept me bound. It took me further and further away from freedom and away from being my authentic self. Having a larger body helped because it was a protection for me; there were very few people who could penetrate the barriers that I had put around myself and my beliefs.

Just how limiting my body weight was throughout most of my life really only became apparent once I moved it!

Finding Freedom...

In 2008 when I was thirty-five I underwent gastric banding. My weight had peaked at just over 120kg and when I went in to be operated on in May 2008 I weighed in at 108kg. Most of my clothes were a size 24/26 and my bras were size 22DD.

Losing weight over the last five years has been an interesting journey for me and brought me closer to freedom and my authentic self than I ever dreamed possible. I have maintained a healthier weight of 65kg over the past three years and feel like I am comfortable in my skin as I am.

I have attached below an article I wrote in 2010 outlining a little of my story. I wrote this piece after completing my Neuro-linguistic Programing (NLP) qualifications and when I was considering going into helping other gastric banding clients:

My story:

After losing over 30kgs in a twelve month period and going from a size 26 to purchasing my first pair of size 12 jeans in more than 25 years one would think I would be on top of the world! It would be easy to assume the new me would be feeling confident, sexy and powerful. I had imagined that all my issues of insecurity, unattractiveness, and incompleteness – in fact all of my issues – would have dropped off with the kilos. Instead I found myself in a very different space.

Looking in the mirror I did not see the new revised slimmer me. I still saw the old me with all my insecurities and insufficiencies. Physically I knew I was smaller, I knew I had more energy, I felt lighter but I didn't feel freer!

Compliments and confirmation from outside me were coming thick and fast.

Everyone noticed how much I had changed, commented on how much better I looked – but it didn't sink in. I heard what they said and I knew they were right but I didn't feel it inside. In fact, if anything I felt less confident! And as strange as it sounds I even felt less sexy.

Who was I now? My whole identity and sense of self had been wrapped up and wrapped around me in excess of 120kgs of weight. I had carried those kilos for more than 20 years; they defined me, made me who I was and provided me with all the reasons I couldn't be what I wanted to be!

*I still walked into my old clothing stores and then felt **disappointed** because all the clothes were too big for me! It was challenging to walk into a "normal" clothing store and then not have to go to the end of the rack with all the oversized garments.*

I still thought that people saw me as a size 26 person who seriously needed to lose weight. I didn't talk to people and I was still not participating fully in life because I was still thinking 'fat'.

One of the most challenging times of all was when I was out for a meal with work colleagues I didn't really know and I could only eat such a small amount on my plate because of my lap-band surgery. When this would happen a tape would start running in my head that went something like this,

"They are looking at me eating such a small amount and thinking 'Yeah right, that fat chick only eats that much, I bet she goes home and eats donuts after this!'"

Another thing I did was carry around a photo of me at 115kg in my bag. I just couldn't let go of the old me. I would bring out the photo and show people almost as a way of making excuses for myself. I was constantly reminding myself of how I used to look – no wonder I couldn't embrace the new me!

After doing a Personal Break-Through session (a four hour Neuro-linguistic Programing intervention) I have been able to release all these limiting beliefs and decisions about myself. I have shed the negative self-talk and negative self-image I had for so many years. I am comfortable in my own skin and not afraid to look at it in the mirror!

NOW I participate 100% in life.

NOW I have no excuses, I know only results.

*NOW I am 100% comfortable in my body as it is **now**!*

NOW I accept and love what I see in the mirror.

NOW I see the real me in the mirror.

NOW the compliments I receive, I receive with gratitude.

NOW I am living the life I want.

NOW I am free to be ME!

NOW I help others release their limiting decisions and beliefs that hold them back from being all they could be NOW!

The above highlights some of the revelations that came from physically releasing the weight from around me.

In October 2010 I had an abdomnoplasty operation (tummy tuck) where the surgeons removed 1.6kg of excess skin! Before I went into the surgery I spent some time doing a visualisation of putting all the words of ridicule, all the limiting beliefs that I had taken up, all the negative self-belief about my body into the excess skin so that it could physically stay on the floor of the surgeon's rooms. I no longer needed it and no longer wanted to carry it around with me!

It was an incredibly freeing experience and it still feels so good to look in the mirror and I honestly look and love what I see reflected back at me!

I often marvel now when my weight fluctuates, as it does with many women on a monthly basis, and I notice 2 or 3 extra kilos. I offer an affirmation of gratitude that I notice this now after so many years of being literally numb to not noticing the changes in my body weight at all. It amazes me just how distanced I was from my feelings.

I will never forget moments of healing once the weight had gone where even though it felt more painful to talk about the abuse, and I felt sadness at a deeper level, I felt happiness more fully because quite literally the layers of protection, all 60+kgs of it, had been removed.

I might add that I also feel the cold now far more than I ever did and have often found myself standing at the train station on a cold Melbourne winter morning wishing for some of that insulation back!

Exercise is another area very much linked to how free I felt within my body. Over the years I have done very little exercise at all. My family's religious beliefs prevented me from playing in any team sport outside of school. I am sure this played a part in my lack of commitment or my freedom to ever consider myself doing any sporting activity seriously. Dancing, singing and drama also fell into this category as well. I made the most of being able to do it at primary school where I played in a netball team and was found participating in the school assembly on a Friday morning most weeks.

Later in life my lack of interest in exercise came purely because I was so unfit and ashamed of my body. I have joined gyms many times throughout my adult life and have also tried swimming regularly but nothing has stuck or worked for me. I had never got to an enjoyment stage with any form of exercise, as it has always been a challenge.

Finding yoga has been amazing. It is the only form of exercise that I have stuck at for more than a month and I am loving it. Even as I write I hear that inner voice, "Well, let's wait and see how long it lasts before you start writing about it in your book eh?" SO that is exactly why I am writing it here; I love yoga and it has become an important part of my life; not just the physical asana practice but I am also enjoying the spiritual practices as well.

This morning I offered an affirmation of gratitude as I was in class and with my eyes closed realised that I was not thinking about what others thought of me, I did not care if I was doing it better or worse than anyone else around me, whether my bum looked fat, or whether the rolls under my arms were showing; I was just loving being on the mat and grateful for my breath!

Freedom to love and accept my body, to treat it with love and respect, to genuinely hold myself tall and proud around others is still a new and exciting development and I am sure that there are still more areas of freedom I can explore in this area of my life.

SELF-LIMITING BELIEFS:

"I am too fat to..."
"I need protection from others"
"I am not safe"
"I am unlovable"
"I am unworthy"

AFFIRMATIONS FOR FREEDOM:

"I love and approve of myself"
"I am enough as I am"
"I am source, all I need is within me now"
'I love and reward myself by making healthy choices"
"I make time to experience myself as myself through yoga and meditation"
"I choose to be in my feeling body"
"I am a healthy spiritual being living my purpose and creating an exceptional life"

Freedom Financially

Financial Freedom – wow, now here's a big topic. There is a whole industry built around the topic; so many people are making lots of money by advising others on how to become financially free.

I'm not there yet but I certainly know what it is like at the opposite end of the spectrum. I also know that I am grateful to not be there now and yet I am aware I still have much to learn.

I grew up with very little in terms of material goods. I honestly didn't realise at the time and probably didn't become aware of it until later in my teenage years.

We lived in state housing, my parents struggled between one good catch of fish and the next, and I think a lot of my memories about the lack of money were not linked to being unable to have it, but more to the notion that spiritually it was wrong. For example, I didn't have the clothes that I wanted because we weren't allowed to wear jeans and t-shirts with writing on it. My sister or mother made most of our clothes. I thought this was because it was hard to buy skirts and suitable clothes that met with the church's standards rather than because we couldn't afford it. We didn't have new cars but I thought this was because Dad was a mechanic and there were five of us kids so we needed a bigger car. We didn't have radios, TVs or stereos and I certainly didn't have electronic games, or go to the movies, or out for dinner, or have make-up, but that was not about money to me; it was about our beliefs. I didn't see us differently from other families at all in a financial way.

In my teenage years, after Dad had died, I became friends with a girl in the church who had money. She came from a wealthy family and although she was older than me I think it was the first time that I started to feel "not as good" on a financial scale. During this time I also acquired my first debt as I had a credit card for the first time and I started to buy clothes that were expensive brand labels like my friend wore. I was about eighteen at the time.

Essentially for the next 10-15 years I struggled with money in similar ways to this, my need to prove myself became more apparent as my sexual acting out became more prominent. I was spending money I did not have on going out drinking in pubs and clubs. I was buying clothes that were very expensive because those around me had clothes that were expensive. I had friends who had less than me as well but it made me feel better because I saw myself as more superior than them. I borrowed money from friends and family and made some incredibly unwise decisions.

In 2004 I declared bankruptcy owing approximately $100K. I was earning $45K per year at the time. I was a single parent and $70K of the debt was mortgaged against my mother's home. It was an extremely low period of my life and a time surrounded by shame and regret to this day for the people this impacted.

I engaged a financial planner to help and advise me as my shame had kept my situation such a secret from others that I felt I had no one to turn to within my circle of friends or family. I was so deep in shame that I could not even acknowledge to myself how far into debt I had gotten myself. I had nothing to show for it except a wardrobe of expensive clothes, memories of many drunken nights out, having sex with many different men and a truckload of shame!

The bankruptcy notice went into the local newspaper on the 11th of September 2003 and for weeks afterwards I walked around with my head hung low. I would look at people and wonder if they knew, had they read the paper, what had they heard, what had they been told, what did they think?? It was excruciating for me, and my family as well. My mother's house was mortgaged and she was on a widow's pension. I had to answer to my brothers and sisters, some of whom didn't know that I had even borrowed against the house as Mum had enabled my secret to that extent.

With the help of my financial planner I worked through the next 12 months, paying back what I could. Whilst I was no longer legally liable for the loan against Mum's house, I was 100% committed to it not ever falling on Mum to pay it back.

At that time I lived in New Zealand as a single parent with my son, who was 9-years-old. My financial planner would deposit $35 into my account each week, which was all I had left over once rent, groceries and bills were paid. In order to go to the doctor I needed to save up for 2 weeks as at that time it cost $50 per visit. It was a time of humiliation, of shame and struggle and not a lot of freedom at all.

It took quite a while to build my way back up out of this situation but I became determined to do so, and I remain grateful to those who helped me out in the process.

I had another experience 2 years later when I found myself without money again, but this time I was in another country, my marriage of less than 2 years was over and I was responsible not just for my 11-year-old son but now I also had a 1-year-old daughter to provide for. This time was different because I had learnt from the past and I knew if I was to get out of this situation it was not about borrowing more money, it was not about relying on anyone else; if it was to be any different I needed to change my thinking and my behaviour.

I had started a new job one week before I found myself and my one year old daughter sleeping in the car. On the Monday morning I went into my new manager and asked for a loan to be able to get a bond together so I could get a place for us to live. Thankfully she obliged and so I was able to have shelter and a home for my two children and me to start afresh. We started again with very little and being in another country meant that there were no financial benefits or avenues available to me so I had to work, and work hard I did. I was the top sales person for the company that year, I worked every minute I could, I travelled far and wide to close deals and I was driven; it became almost about life and death for me!

Four months after I started my new job I had my salary review and my manager doubled my base salary!

I had known and experienced as much as I ever wanted to of financial lack or bondage; I was intent on creating freedom for my children and myself.

Finding Freedom...

Eight years on and I have gone from sleeping in my car to a recent job earning $200K a year and travelling all over Australia. My husband and I now own our own home and we have a couple of vehicles between us; they are a lot more comfortable than the one I had to sleep in eight years ago too might I add!

Changing my beliefs about money and the lack of money has been important for me to get to where I am now. And yet there have been many layers of learning for me around financial freedom and my attitude towards money and status. Earning a lot financially, having a great title on your business card, excellent opportunities and achievement doesn't necessarily bring freedom and/or happiness. It does certainly bring choice though.

This was the next layer of awareness for me. I had made it financially, was earning more than many of my associates and earned more than I had dreamed I would and yet I was not happy. In part I believe this was because I grew up with a belief that "money doesn't buy you happiness" and also because I had created for myself another level of bondage. I was in a role, in an industry and in a position that I was good at; that I was capable of and even excelling at, and yet I was not happy and I still felt like something was missing!

Therein lay the motivator behind my three months of what I refer to as my "Eat, Pray, Love" when I was 40-years-old. Ninety days of exploring the inner me, the beliefs that I was born into, the beliefs that have developed through experience and that I had unconsciously taken on as my own. These included the belief that there is never enough money, the belief that our family will never be rich, that you have to work hard for everything in life. That a woman's place in the home, that men are the providers of the family, and ultimately, that money doesn't buy you happiness. All of these beliefs were preventing me from financial freedom and freedom in my career.

Going into business for myself and doing something completely different to the sales and corporate life that I have been in for the past 15-20 years has been one of the most rewarding and life changing experiences of my life. Remarkably, life coaching and Reiki have brought incredible freedom in all aspects of my life and they incorporate all the transferable skills that my life experience has given me. They have brought me as much in terms of financial benefits as any of my corporate sales roles and in addition to this they have enhanced my happiness, gratitude and contentment with my life.

I trust I will never forget these periods of my life of having no freedom around money. I intend to look back on these experiences with gratitude because they have given me an appreciation of freedom that comes from not being bound by debt, and paying off the mortgage on my mother's house in the past 12 months validated this for me.

SELF-LIMITING BELIEFS:

"Money is the root of all evil"

"Money cannot buy you happiness"

"You'll never be rich – you're a (insert your family name in here)"

"The more money you have the more problems and temptations"

AFFIRMATIONS FOR FREEDOM:

"I love and attract money"

"Money is a source of happiness"

"I choose to live debt free – I pay any debts willingly and easily"

"I consciously connect to the universal flow of abundance"

"I am source, all I need is within me now"

"I give thanks my self-worth is no longer determined by my material possessions"

Freedom To Dream

Dreaming is one of the places where our subconscious mind really has an opportunity to experience freedom without any obvious consequence. When I was a child my dreams were very limited due to the constraints around right and wrong and what I was encouraged to believe was possible for me.

Because of my belief and understanding that God knows all our thoughts, the risk of upsetting Him and angering Him with our evil thoughts was very restricting. To dream of having a nicer car, a bigger house, a better bike or anything bigger or better was considered being envious and envy was not a trait I wanted to be known for, or even to acknowledge within myself. To dream of wanting clothes like the other girls was to want to be worldly and that would upset God. I knew there were some clothes and many other things that were just out of the realm of my parents ever allowing me to have or buy, and so I learnt to not even allow myself to think or wish for such things.

Interestingly as mentioned before this was not equated to money in my mind or whether we could afford it – it was simply that "good girls" or "God's people" did not have such things. In fact my understanding was that God's people should not even want these things.

I remember sneaking out and going to the movies to see "Annie" when I was about 11 or 12 years old with my friends. The guilt and fear I experienced, not only of Mum and Dad finding out, but thinking that God might come back to earth and find me in the movie theatre was so real and frightening that I came to believe that I was wrong and evil for wanting these things. And as is the way of life, the guilt and shame I felt when I did want these things was all the evidence I needed.

The restrictions of the initial religious beliefs stayed with me for many years; despite no longer attending the church I found it challenging to dream or to believe that I was worthy of more.

I recall another memory that serves as evidence of my restrictions around dreaming. We were brought up with the belief that a marriage on earth was important but not as significant as being the "Bride of Christ" at the end of time. As a result, women were not to wear white on their wedding day and weddings were a relatively quiet event in comparison to traditional weddings. I recall at 10- or 11-years-old when Princess Diana and Prince Charles were married, and whilst marvelling at the beauty of Diana, the dress and the ceremony, it never ever entered my head to ever dream of being a princess at my own wedding.

When I got married the first time, I was 32-years-old, I was 110kg and I was living within the religious belief again, although I married a man who wasn't. We had twelve people at our wedding in the Botanic Gardens followed by an afternoon tea at my mother's place. I wore a black top with a silver print on it and my aunt made me a long silver skirt. It was a modest affair for many reasons. The first was that we didn't have a lot of money in addition to marrying someone not in the church so we were met with judgement, and lastly was because I was a single parent and therefore obviously tainted material to begin with. We were married in a hurry because my fiancé had been offered work in another town and my belief prevented us living together before marriage so we decided to get married quickly and move together. It was a beautiful day and certainly all that I believed I deserved at the time.

Roll the clock forward to when I got married seven years later – I was 39-years-old, I now weighed 65kg; I was no longer living in the religious belief, and now had three children. I had done a lot of work on myself and my beliefs and made many changes to my life, both internally and externally. However, when it came to getting ready for the wedding up surfaced my limiting beliefs and the inability to dream big! Thankfully my husband to be this time around had no restrictions about such things.

My initial thoughts when it came to my dress were that I would find a style that suited me and my new size and shape and then get something made for me. I went to visit my sister as she is a fantastic dressmaker and wonderfully honest with me about such things and we decided to go and have a look at some bridal shops to find a style that might suit me.

At 39-years-old I had never looked in a shop quite like a bridal shop ever! Mainly because I had no need and going from a size 26 just two years before it was unlikely I would find anything in my size in such a store. Just walking into the store was taking me beyond any dreaming I had done before. The next stage of looking at dresses to try on was interesting too.

Firstly I was looking for a colour – my mind assured me that at 39-years-old and with three children there was no way I could wear a white dress so I was thinking of a turquoise blue colour. Then there was the limit I had put on myself that I needed to have sleeves to cover my arms and certainly my shoulders!

Meanwhile my sister and the retail assistant were pulling out dresses that they believed would suit my shape and size and their selection was not hindered by my internal dialogue of self-doubt and limitations! It was extremely confronting to me as I looked at the gowns I had selected hanging beside the ones they had chosen. I fussed about, attempted to make excuses and in vain tried to get them to understand the limits of my mind. Thankfully they challenged me and got me to have some fun, and to just trust them for a bit.

I will never forget trying on that first beautiful white wedding gown – which of course was the one I was married in 12 months later – and standing in front of the mirror! Seeing myself reflected in the mirror – a size 12, shoulders showing, in a white gown and looking like a princess. It was beyond anything I had ever dreamed of before.

This was a turning point for me in terms of our forthcoming nuptials and so I allowed myself to plan and experience a wedding far beyond and more wonderful than my wildest expectations! My motto became, "You only get married the *second* time once".

There are many other instances as I reflect now of how my internal dialogue, my internal fears and beliefs have prevented me from dreaming too big.

Finding Freedom...

Coming into a place where I was willing and able to really reflect and challenge my unconscious beliefs, explore them without judgement or regret, was a pivotal moment for me in finding freedom. This included exploring my spirituality and my long-held beliefs through the guidance of my life coach and spending time in meditation and reflection.

Holding my new belief that I am whom I choose to be and that I am creating my experience with every thought, word and action has been instrumental in me examining my dreams and how big they are!

I realise now without a doubt that I have achieved, created and received everything I have believed I am worthy of. My potential in life is equal to my beliefs and dreams for myself, less my fears, so making time to dream and to build the belief in myself is essential.

I have achieved a lot in my life despite not dreaming big or believing I am worthy of very much! I am often reminded of just how far I have come and the success I have known and I feel a sense of gratitude and pride when I reflect on this. Becoming a parent to the wonderful children I have, the loving relationship, the amazing career and awesome opportunities that have been afforded to me, living in another country, being the size I am now and having my health is truly a gift and certainly there have been times where I never dreamed such things were possible for me.

I can't help now but wonder just how life could get better than this? As I allow myself now to consciously dream big and with the awareness that I am who I choose to be!

Each day I spend time meditating and affirming that my thoughts and my dreams are positive, they are aligned with my purpose and they are big. I figure given all the evidence I have in my own personal life that my dreams do come true, then I want to make them good ones and BIG!

SELF-LIMITING BELIEFS:

"I am not worthy".
"I don't deserve".
"I can't".

AFFIRMATIONS FOR FREEDOM:

"I am constantly creating".
"I am worthy".
"I am enough as I am".
"I am source, all I need is within me now".
"I dream big and all of my dreams come true".

Freedom To Speak My Truth

"You need to learn to bite your tongue young lady!" "If you haven't got anything nice to say then don't say it." "Be careful what you say – your words can come back to bite you." "You'll end up eating your words." "Ask yourself – Is it true, is it necessary and is it kind before you say anything."

These were all the strong messages that surrounded me from a very young age and ones that have good intent behind them - when they are in context.

As a contradiction to all of these messages, I was constantly told when I was younger that I had the gift of the gab. One of my grandparents even said I had been vaccinated by a gramophone needle! My father's father was a talker, as was my father and it would seem that I inherited their ability to tell a good yarn and to speak confidently.

During my early schooling years one would often find me on stage come assembly time, creating plays and skits. I was an avid writer too, getting 'A grades' in

English, writing stories, diaries and poems. Writing was an avenue I often used to express the words I was unable to say out loud about thoughts I had that didn't align with a "good girl" or a "Child of God". I made a pact with my sister when I was younger that if I ever died she was to find my diaries and burn them before Mum or anyone else ever got a chance to read them!

There was an often quoted saying that I heard a lot growing up – I am not sure if it was a family thing, a belief thing or maybe it was wider than that. The quote was "Children should be seen and not heard". Whilst in its strictest sense this was not upheld within the family, when it came to deeper serious topics it was an underlying belief that meant that while I was a child (or if I was younger than you) then what I had to say didn't hold as much weight as if an adult said it, or if it came from someone my elder.

I spent a fair bit of time in my early high school years in the corridor outside the classroom for being disruptive in class. Most of my reports throughout school suggest I could do a lot better in my grades if I spent more time applying myself rather than socialising and talking in class.

Therefore one of my greatest gifts – as I recognise it now – was not encouraged or welcomed whilst I was growing up. I was the chatterbox, the jabber jaws, and the noisy one. My older brother and sister still joke about how they used to bribe me with lollies on long car trips if I could keep quiet for more than 5 minutes!

Not sure how many of those lollies I actually got to claim either to be honest!

Whilst in many instances I was not afraid to ask questions of others in my attempts to understand people and situations more, I intuitively knew what secrets I had to keep and that some things were not up for questioning. These were namely my sexual abuse, which I never discussed with anyone because of the threats from my grandfather, but it was also about the shame that was attached to it. I also knew not to question too much about our beliefs because if I did then the explanation I got back was along the lines that one's level of faith determines one's level of questioning therefore my questions showed a lack of faith. A lack of faith was not something to be proud of!

On reflection I also see that questions of why we did certain things, or were not allowed to do certain things when I was younger, were answered with verses from the bible or what the preachers had preached from the platform. By the time I was older I had stopped asking the questions out loud as it had become just a part of life and to admit to questioning it would show my lack of faith even more.

The truth is I got to the point of not even asking the questions internally and as is the case with our human existence, our belief system is created not necessarily on what we believe for ourselves but what the beliefs are of those around us. I think one of these beliefs that limited me the most throughout my life was what I saw reflected around me so often – "If it is not spoken about, it is not happening".

You could say that my gift of speech got me into a lot of trouble. I would find words coming out of my mouth at times that I wasn't quite sure where they came from, for what the reason and/or the consequences would prove to be!

One of those moments was when I came out and told my mother about the sexual abuse when I was fourteen. It was not planned, I didn't fully understand what the purpose of telling her was, nor what I expected her response to be. It came out one day when we were discussing living with my grandparents for a few months while our house sold and the rest of the family moved towns. I blurted out that I didn't want to live with them so Grandad could play around with me again. I recall Mum taking a deep breath, looking at me quizzically and then telling me not to be so stupid and that I needed to learn to behave myself and fit in. Nothing more was mentioned by either of us about this for another five years when I started therapy.

Keeping secrets was something I learnt how to do very young in life and I have managed to keep many secrets over the years – for other people, about other people and most damaging of all are the ones I have kept from, and about myself. This came under the guise of being a good Christian and not causing pain to others, of not upsetting the apple cart or getting involved in other people's business! Once again the clear obvious message was that if we don't give voice to something it will go away, and if it is not talked about it's not happening.

I now see that this ability to express myself both via written and oral words has been one of the biggest gifts of my life and really the path that has ensured I know the freedom in my life that I know now.

Finding Freedom…

Since coming out and talking about the abuse there have been many experiences through my life where my gift of expression and speaking my truth has brought freedom – not just to myself but also to others. Whilst it was me who came out and told of the sexual abuse of my grandfather more than 20 years ago, I'd like to think speaking my truth has allowed others a choice to speak theirs too.

I also believe that by bringing it to the awareness of family and the elders of the church at the time; ultimately gave Grandad some freedom for himself as well in his final few years of life. I can only imagine the burden that this secret must have been on him and the energy he would have consumed keeping it hidden and ensuring that all his victims kept it a secret too. Unfortunately, other than a letter of apology and admission of guilt written by Grandad to his children, and also a personal one to me before his death, I will not know this for sure.

On another occasion in my teenage years I was the one who told a woman that her husband was having an affair, and that all of his family, many of hers and most of their friends were aware of the affair but no one had told her. I have been the spokesperson on many family issues that have arisen throughout my life where I have made people accountable for their actions and identified how these actions impacted on others. I have voiced concerns over suspected abuse of children; and have also had challenging conversations with elders of my family and the church throughout the years as well. My ability and freedom to speak my truth has also been prominent in my professional career and certainly in my success as a sales person. I have learnt that being honest and speaking my truth brings great success in sales and life in general.

Many of these experiences have come at a great cost – or it would seem that way from the outside looking in. I have lost friendships, have been misunderstood and judged harshly and wrongly by many in my family. I have been disconnected from the church, which obviously was my whole social, emotional and physical world growing up. I have lost sales because I couldn't lie. I have had many changes in my management roles because I have not been prepared to intentionally mislead or play the political game that often comes with corporate management.

I think the ultimate affront came when standing at the foot of my grandfather's bed where he lay dead, when I was asked, "Don't you feel guilty about what you put him through in the last few years of his life?"

So yes, the freedom to speak my truth doesn't come easily or without consequence, however each time it has brought a new level of appreciation, peace and freedom.

To be perfectly honest I now **choose** to live honouring and speaking my truth to the best of my ability each day because I firmly believe it is my purpose and my soul's work to do so.

I also appreciate the truth behind the words, "If you don't speak about it then it is not happening!" I now see it all in the context of creation and I have a full appreciation of the power that our words add to our beliefs and desires. So I speak freely about what is happening in my world that I am creating – without shame I speak my truth out loud, I speak my goals and dreams out loud, I speak affirmations and love out loud and I shout my joy from the roof tops as loudly as I possibly can because it's true – if I don't give it voice then it won't happen!

This book is the next layer of speaking my truth. I appreciate as I sit here and write I am potentially opening myself up to more misunderstanding and judgement from those who have different memories or views to mine. However, I know that by writing this book I am also opening myself up to a greater experience of freedom for myself. I write this book also with the full intent that in doing so I allow others who read this book, and even those whose lives are touched by those who read this book, an avenue to access freedom for themselves as well.

SELF-LIMITING BELIEFS:

"Children should be seen and not heard"
"If you don't speak about it – then it is not happening"

AFFIRMATIONS FOR FREEDOM:

"I give thanks for my freedom to speak my truth and follow my heart"

Afterword...
Freedom Through Gratitude

After completing the writing of this account of how I found freedom and whilst it was going through the first round of edits, I took a week's holiday. I called it my "Gratitude Journey" and I went back, on my own, to the country of my birth – New Zealand.

It was a remarkable journey on so many levels and I was blessed in every sense of the word. I chose to revisit old partners who I had not seen for 15-17 years. I went back to the treatment centre where I spent 12 weeks as an in-house resident twenty years previously. I visited the graveside, for the first time since his death, 20 years ago, of my grandfather who had abused me. I even took him flowers.

I walked and drove around the streets of the town where I grew up. I knocked on the door of the house I spent eleven years of my childhood and had my photo taken on the front steps. I sat under the same tree in the Botanical Gardens where I had my first kiss with a boy when I was 11-years-old. I revisited many of the beaches, rivers and locations that we used to go as a family for a "Sunday drive". I caught up with good friends who have been instrumental in my growth and who have had an impact in my life in some way or another.

Given that the trip was only recent, I am sure that I still haven't acknowledged all of the blessings, lessons and revelations that the trip held for me but I want to complete this book by sharing my initial ones:

Our peripheral vision expands and everything looks beautiful when looking from a base point of gratitude.

While it had been five years since I'd been home to New Zealand and after living in Australia for nine years, I anticipated that the countryside would look so much lusher and greener. What I did not realise or appreciate was just how beautiful **every-thing** and **every-one** looks when I am feeling grateful. Also just how much I would see and notice, as if for the first time, to be grateful for.

I laughed and sang out loud as I walked in the rain – 3 of the mornings I was there I chose to go out for a walk despite the fact that it was raining. I felt grateful for the sensation of the refreshing rain on my face. I felt grateful as I walked for my fitness and the fact that I had the energy to even go for a walk. Many of the places where I walked I physically could not have done so when I was 65kg heavier.

The rivers where I swam as a child were so clear and beautiful, I noticed the birds as they flew along the edge of the river, I noticed their chirping, the sound of bumble bees as they collected nectar from the flowers.

As I flew from one city to another, over the countryside I noticed the beauty of the hills, the valleys, the mountains and the bush. No one thing was better or worse than the other – the hills as beautiful as the plains, the valleys as important as the mountain peaks.

The difference of opinions of the people I met from my past was beautiful as well. I was grateful that our friendships were solid enough and based on enough love that we could argue our points, stand up for our beliefs and yet not get upset or take it personally. I was grateful that from my newfound place of freedom I didn't feel I had to conform – neither did I feel they should either. I experienced and loved them with gratitude and this created an energy of freedom for them to be themselves as well.

I noticed the manhole covers on the streets of Wellington, which had New Zealand Maori designs on them. I noticed the aging on some precious faces of those I love, I noticed that my Grandfather was 82 years old when he died and I noticed the change in the colours of the trees. I noticed it all from a space of love and a place of gratitude, which only served to intensify the beauty of each and every thing.

I noticed things that had not changed and I noticed things that had. I appreciated things as if seeing them for the very first time and essentially I was!

When I choose to approach life from a base of gratitude then I create an environment of love and freedom that allows everything around me to be its authentic self.

Each and every one of us is at our most beautiful when we feel the freedom to be our authentic self.

When judging myself I take account of my values, beliefs and thoughts as well as my actions and behaviours. When judging others I only judge them by their actions and behaviours.

On the night I left Australia I posted a photo of myself on Facebook of when I was in rehab 20 years earlier. It was not a flattering photo at all. When I looked at it I saw a confused, sad, lonely, lost and mixed up addicted version of myself. My purpose for posting the photo was to show the vast comparison of who I was then and who I am now.

I made the comment that the first person I would see in New Zealand had not seen me since this time and I wondered if he would recognise me! The person who would meet me was actually my fiancé at the time the picture was taken.

I was taken aback when he mentioned the photo not long into our meeting. He admonished me for posting the photo and for my insinuating in the post that there was something wrong with who I was or how I looked in the photo. This was particularly confronting for me and it took some discussing for me to understand where he was coming from.

When I looked at the photo of me I saw the whole picture of me – the inside and the out. I recalled how I felt about myself; I knew how confused, sad, lonely and ashamed I was about life at the time and when I looked at the photo that is what I saw. I physically looked very different on the outside; I was not smiling, was overweight and smoking a cigarette. My intention of posting the photo came from a place of comparison. As I looked at the photo I compared it to how I feel now, what I believe about myself now, what I understand about life now, as well as how I look and act outwardly now.

What he told me he saw when he looked at the photo was the woman he loved. The woman who was going through a tough time but that had shown him love, that was and is a great mother to her son, and the woman who at that time he was planning to marry and spend the rest of his life with.

What I had not considered was that my judgement of myself includes the 80% of what others cannot see or know, that is, what I am thinking and feeling at the time. The way I experience myself and my life is based around my values and beliefs as well as my actions and behaviours. What others experience of me is only 20% of who I am. They can only know me through my actions and behaviours. Ultimately my actions and behaviours are governed by my values and beliefs but they are not so easy to understand – especially when most of them are unconscious.

I also realised that what others experienced or judged me from was a basis of their own values and beliefs. It was through these lenses that they judged my actions and behaviours.

As I look back through this book with this deeper awareness I see clearly the many times I adjusted my actions and behaviours against my own values and beliefs. I did this most times because it was what I believed others expected of me, or based on what I thought would make them happy.

A great example of life – two people see the same photo but two totally different interpretations. As is with life, many of us are subject to the same events and yet our experience of it can be vastly different.

This is a reaffirmation for me as I conclude the writing of this book – this is my experience of my life, the way I have experienced all of these things in my life.

I cannot expect others who lived alongside me to necessarily have the same memories or to have had the same experience.

'My beliefs and perception of my experiences shapes my reality regardless of how accurate it is.'

I sat around the table with a friend of more than 35 years that I went to school with and who was a part of my life as I was adopting many of my lifetime beliefs about myself. She has continued to drop into my life throughout the years for which I am extremely grateful. Her sister (who is 6-7 years older than us) called in to visit and the three of us were in a deep discussion – it had been more than 10 years since we had sat down and had a "real" conversation with each other, and even longer than that with her sister. I was sharing with them the writing of this book, and about the purpose of my trip home.

I mentioned the lack of freedom I experienced through my childhood by my religious upbringing and having to be so different in what I wore, where I went, how I looked and ultimately being the only one in school who had these restrictions. I sat incredulously at the table as my friend turned to me and said, "What do you mean? You were always just Maria. We never considered any of those things about you. You were just Maria, my good friend, you were always loving and fun."

Incredibly her sister spoke up then and said, "I didn't even know you guys were religious".

How confronting was that moment for my identity? My whole perception of my childhood was challenged in that moment.

What did this mean?

My reality, and therefore the way I experienced my life, has not been accurate!

All those years thinking that **everyone** was judging me, that they all thought I was different and weird. From this basis I created a belief that I was not free to be myself, that I was not OK just as I am, that I was different and I didn't measure up.

The result of this thinking and belief system has meant that I have created a life of actions and behaviours that have confirmed and validated this distorted reality.

(I acknowledge here that I didn't have this conversation with **everyone** and no doubt there were some people who didn't see me as my friend did).

Imagine if I had chosen another map of reality for myself – if I had chosen to believe that I was enough as I am? Or if I had believed the same as what my friend did – that I was just Maria – I was a good friend and I was loving and fun?

It is simply my judgement and perception of events, of situations and experiences that creates my reality. Unless I have the courage to challenge myself, to explore my self-limiting beliefs, to take the time and energy it requires to bring my long-held beliefs into my conscious awareness and take ownership for them then nothing can change.

And that is exactly what I am choosing now – through uncovering, discovering, challenging and exploring my unconscious self-limiting beliefs about myself, I am now creating the life I choose to live and love.

I am choosing to live my life with freedom – being grateful for the gift in every experience.

And so it is – and may it also be for anyone who chooses the same.
With Gratitude and Freedom
Maria

Photo Gallery

The Buller River, Tip Head and the bar where Dad's boat was over-turned in 1985. (photo taken in 2014)

Standing on the tip head where my school friend, stood as Dad's boat was overturned by the freak wave.
Photo taken in 2014

Memorial at Tip Head of Westport harbour.

Dads grave – photo taken 2014

Outside the bedroom window of our old house – in 1985 (after Dad died) .and then again in 2014

Outside and Springhill Rehab in
Napier – 2014

On the porch in rehab 1995 (22 years old)

Same porch – 2014 (42 years old)

2014 First visit to Grandad's grave to lay
flowers since his death in 1993
– an experience of gratitude and forgiveness

Me Post Rehab in 1995

2015 on completion of this book
"Living with FreedOm" after FACING MARIA

Printed in the United States
By Bookmasters